Dairy Free Keto Cookbook

*The Complete Beginner's Guide
to Dairy Free Keto*

Table of Contents

direct or indirect, which are incurred as a result of the use of information contained within this document, including, but not limited to, —errors, omissions, or inaccuracies.

Introduction

First of all, I would love to thank you purchasing this book'
Dairy Free keto cookbook'! I hope you find it is interesting and
that it helps you with the keto diet.

We live in a day and age when there is a lot of focus on
staying fit and leading a healthy lifestyle. It is more than just
a personal aim to constantly maintain being at our fittest,
whether we are 17 or 70!

Everyone has their own reason as to why they want to go on a
diet – it could be anything from weight loss to an overall fit
lifestyle. But then they are obstructed by doubts – is it worth
it to give up on the foods they love?

Well, fret not! This book has been crafted especially for your
needs and to remove whatever doubts you might be having.
Contained within the chapters, you will find ample amounts
of information detailing what the ketogenic diet is and how
you can benefit from it, along with why dairy-free is such a
good idea.

This diet, along with its dairy-free aspect, has gained
immense popularity and all for the right reasons. It is
recommended by experts all around the world because of the
innumerable ways the human body benefits from it. Apart
from all the valuable information, you will also find dairy-
free keto recipes that will catapult you into your dairy-free
keto journey.

Thank you once again for choosing this book.

Chapter One: The Ketogenic Diet

The Ketogenic diet in its simplest definition is a diet that has low carbohydrate content and, in contrast, a much higher content of fat. It is also commonly referred to as the LCHF diet - low carb, high fat.

In the keto diet, the dietary expectation of you is to make sure your intake of protein rich foods is appropriate, as this is the very foundation of the diet. There was a time when it was used as a treatment method for many types of ailments and diseases, whereas currently, it has garnered vast amounts of popularity for its effectiveness in weight loss, especially for those who are taking up the keto diet specifically to lose weight.

All around the world, it is being hailed by experts and specialists as the diet that can change your life with the smallest of alterations made in your dietary habits and lifestyle.

Normally, what happens in your body is that it burns carbohydrates in order to generate energy for you to function on. While on the keto diet, fats do the job of being the primary source of energy. Any person with a normal diet ends up consuming enormous quantities of carbohydrates, be it as a choice or something they consider to be the general approach to diets. But it is important to note that when carbohydrates are converted into glucose, the vast amounts of carbs turn into outrageous amounts of glucose that are released into your bloodstream, which in turn leads to weight gain.

This is where the ketogenic diet steps in. The replacement of carbohydrates with fats turns them into ketones. And in turn – ketones become the principal energy source. You will read about the innumerous health benefits of the ketogenic diet in the upcoming segments of this book.

Keto and its Types

There isn't just one – there are many types of ketogenic diets. Some of the common forms are:

- **High-Protein Ketogenic Diet:** In this diet, the protein quantity dominates the rest of the components of the diet.

- **Targeted Ketogenic Diet (TKD):** Here you are permitted to include carbohydrates in the diet with the condition that you engage in an intense and regular workout regime.

- **Standard Ketogenic Diet (SKD):** This diet's standard meal is supposed to consist of 5% carbs, 75% fat, and 20% proteins.

- **Cyclical Ketogenic Diet (CKD):** Intake days that are high in carbohydrates are allowed.

Chapter Two: Ketosis and the Science behind It

Ketosis

Our body sources its energy from glucose. Glucose is a form of sugar that is produced by sugars and dietary carbohydrates. These include:

- Sugar: foods like fruit and dairy
- Anything high in starch: noodles, rice, wheat and fries, etc.

Upon consumption, your body breaks down the carbohydrates into simple sugars. This is also the category of sugars glucose belongs to, and it is instantly used as fuel for your body. Either that, or it stores up in the liver, and that stored up glucose is a chemical that is known as glycogen.

When the generated amount of glucose falls short to meet your body's need for energy, the body shifts its focus to sourcing the required energy from other ways. One of the main methods includes the breakdown of fat stored in the body and assembling glucose straight from triglycerides. This way of functioning of our body leads to the release ketones. And the process of releasing ketones is called ketosis.

Ketones

Ketones are a type of acid. They accumulate in your body as it goes through the process of ketosis.

They act as a sign of the successful breaking down of fats and the body entering ketosis.

But it is worthy to note that ketones in excess amounts could impact your body in a negative manner and result in a condition known as ketoacidosis.

To Enter Ketosis

Reaching ketosis is not a difficult process although, it might get very confusing for most people, as there is a lot of information on this matter. Here's how ketosis can be attained properly.

Your consumption of carbohydrates being restricted is the most essential aspect of attaining ketosis. In fact, it is also the most vital factor of the keto diet itself. Here, there are two things to be kept in mind:

- Focus on the total carbs
- Focus on the net carbs

The goal is to stay below 35 g of total carbs and 20g of net carbs, per day.

A restriction on your intake of protein is also just as important as restricting your carb intake.

Contrary to the misconception of a lot of people, a high consumption of protein is not necessary as that could lead to weakening the impacts of ketosis. In order to keep a daily check and track of your nutrient levels, consider using ketogenic diet calculators.

Some Important Points to Note:

- Working out helps amplify whatever effects the keto diet could have on your body.
- Fast over starve – fasting can be an effective tool when it comes to spike up your ketone levels and helps keep them engaged all day long.
- Stay hydrated no matter what. You should drink at least a gallon of water on a daily basis. A gallon should be the minimum! Not only that, but drinking water helps in controlling hunger levels as well,
- Consume the required supplements – when you are on a keto diet, if you feel any kind of weakness in your body, it is advisable you consider opting for vitamins, minerals, etc. supplements.
- Frequent snacking – when on a keto diet, this is strongly advised against as that could lead to a spike in insulin levels and it would reduce the effects that help in weight loss.

Identifying the Ketosis Effects

There are several chemical changes, a series of them, happening in your body when the ketosis process occurs.

If left uninitiated, it will become tough to recognize the changes and you may not figure out that ketosis has started in your body. Some of the common characteristics of the effects are the following:

Appetite Suppression

When you only eat vegetables and proteins throughout the keto diet, you will experience your appetite reducing and suppressing itself. This is great for anyone who has issues like frequent snacking, etc.

Loss of Weight

At first, you will experience a lot of weight loss, really fast. This quick dive in your weight is the result of the store of carbohydrates in your body being used up. After this phase of rapid weight loss, it will slow down. It will turn into a slow but sure process, and it is very consistent if you keep following the keto diet properly. Also be sure to keep a check on your calories.

Keto Fever

There is a possibility you will start feeling sick, tired and experience a little brain fog. But fret not – it is a temporary effect. This happens solely because the body starts burning its stores of fat, unlike its previous, regular routine of using carbs as a source of energy. Once you get used to your new routine of no-carbs, your body's level of sugar will stabilize to an extent where it helps eliminate whatever keto fever symptoms you are going through.

Bad Breath

This is probably one of the most eminent symptoms when you enter ketosis. Your breath might adapt an odor that is kind of fruity, as a direct result of the ketone levels increasing. The reason behind that is a kind of ketone, which can be found in your urine and also your breath. This kind of ketone is called acetone.

Even if it may seem like an antagonist to your social life, this effect of bad breath is, in fact, a good symptom that your diet is progressing the right way. To combat this effect, you can chew gum, but make sure you check the listed ingredients.

Chapter Three: How Keto Affects and Benefits Your Body

Manages Blood Sugar Levels

As mentioned earlier, carbohydrates are the reason behind glucose being released into your bloodstream. This is why consuming carbohydrates instantly results in your levels of energy surging up. The hormone insulin regulates your levels of blood sugar. But for some people, insulin functions in a different way. It fails to regulate the levels of blood sugar and that leads to Type II Diabetes. When insulin fails to function the way it is supposed to, it is called insulin resistance.

So, in the case of you being resistant to insulin, the keto diet can greatly help relieve the risk of Type II Diabetes. This is directly a result of the sugar amount releasing into the bloodstream because you reduced your consumption of carbs. So even in the scenario of your insulin failing to do its job, there will be no reason for you to worry over Type II Diabetes.

Even if someone is suffering from Type II Diabetes, they can take up this diet as it will help manage it and you will require a minimal amount of medication.

Blood Pressure Levels Being Regulated

Hypertension has turned into a common issue in the households of many lately. It also increases the risk of a lot disorders and they can be related to cardiac, kidney disorders, and some others. As a result, it is impossible not to acknowledge the seriousness of hypertension.

Reducing one's consumption of salt is one of the most commonly prescribed suggestions by physicians, in order to treat hypertension - all because salt can be instrumental in the increase of your levels of blood pressure.

Wait! Before you feel disheartened at the prospect of removing salt from your diet or having to put up with salt-less food, read on ahead –

With the keto diet, your blood sugar levels will be managed without you having to reduce your salt intake in any manner.

Here's how it works:

- Your levels of blood sugar increase by default, as a result of the consumption of foods that are high in carbohydrates. If you are resistant to insulin and your blood sugar levels are surging up, the outcome is your blood vessels getting constricted. This directly impacts your levels of blood pressure and nudges it to rise up. A reduction in your intake of carbohydrates helps manage your blood sugar levels. There is hardly any reason to worry about hypertension or blood vessels getting constricted when you have brought your blood sugar levels under control.
- Insulin resistance is another crucial reason of hypertension. Soon it will be explained to you how all the visceral fat stocked up in your body can be reduced with the help of the keto diet. Reducing the visceral fat amounts helps manage your resistance towards

insulin, which in turn helps lower any factors of risk involved in some cardiac disorders. Managing your insulin resistance means the reduction of one factor of risk in the case of hypertension.

- As you are already aware, your body is encouraged to burn its stores of fat on this diet. When this burning takes place, the potassium and sodium present in your kidneys are cleansed out. This leads to an imbalance of electrolytes, and that can be remedied by increasing your consumption of chicken broth and salt. As must be apparent to you by now, this diet helps manage hypertension without nudging you to reduce your salt intake.

Triglyceride Levels are reduced

An increase in the amount of triglycerides existing in the bloodstream by default ups the risks for many cardiac related disorders. The more you consume carbohydrates, the more the triglyceride levels will go up. As you are aware, carbs convert into glucose and are channeled into your bloodstream as the source of energy.

When there is an excessive amount of glucose in your bloodstream, although the body has already sourced its energy, then the pancreas secretes insulin, which converts the excess but residual glucose into what we call triglycerides.

These then travel to the fat cells. When you aren't consuming foods, the body sources its energy from the store of triglycerides that are released.

Simply put – increased intake of carbohydrates makes way to the levels of triglycerides being increased.

Removal of Visceral Fat

When the foods you have consumed are digested, the fat settles in various parts of your body. This is quite risky because depending on the location of the fat deposits; the factors of risk will tend to vary. Upon consumption the fats are stored in two different places - subcutaneous fat is the fat that is deposited under your skin and visceral fat that is stored on your stomach.

Out of the two, you need to be very careful about visceral fat. It is really dangerous and can negatively affect the quality of the life you are leading. It can also impact the way your organs tend to function. If the amount of visceral fat stored in your body increases, it can lead to organ inflammation, metabolism impairment, and also insulin resistance.

When your metabolism is attacked, it could also affect and negate the efforts you are putting into losing weight. In fact, it could slow down the entire process of weight loss. And that is why it is so important to ensure your deposits of visceral fat are manageable.

The keto diet helps reduce the amount of visceral fat that gets stored up in your body as the diet forces the body to digest this stubborn fat to source energy from. When you get rid of the excess amounts of visceral fat, you automatically reduce the factors of risk for many health disorders. It also stops your weight loss efforts from being rendered useless due to the presence of this fat.

The keto diet is capable of reducing the visceral fat stored in our bodies. This stubborn fat is digested by the body to derive energy. By getting rid of excess visceral fat, you are actually reducing your risk factors of various health disorders. Your efforts to lose weight will also not be compromised by visceral fat's unwanted presence.

Appetite Regulation

This is one of the best aspects of the keto diet – it does not make you feel like you're starving, at least, after the first initial days, once your body starts getting accustomed to sourcing its energy from fat. As a result of this burning of fat to fuel the body, you start feeling more energetic, and the high content of fat in the diet, ensures you are always feeling full.

The keto diet never lets you feel like you are actually on any kind of a diet as it allows you to have all of your favorite foods, with the exception of carbohydrates (and in the case of this book – dairy, as well).

The thing about fats is that it takes time to digest, as opposed to carbohydrates; which is why you end up not feeling hungry too often.

When you are on a carbohydrate specific diet, like any regular diet, your body ends up burning all those carbs really quick and, as a result, you find yourself victimized by frequent hunger pangs.

By following the keto diet, you are eliminating the chances of random and frequent hunger pangs, not to mention the regulation of your appetite also helps in weight loss. Because you are feeling hungry less often, this means eating less than you are used to.

As a result, your only concern becomes reduced burning amounts of calories.

Helps Increase HDL cholesterol level

High Density Lipoprotein is also referred to as good cholesterol. Its job is to ensure that the cholesterol from your food intake goes into the liver. Upon reaching the liver, the cholesterol is either removed from the body or used again by it to derive energy from.

So, HDL cholesterol is instrumental in making sure the content of cholesterol in your food does not clog and create obstructions in our arteries.

As per specific studies, HDL can also be useful in the reduction of inflammation. There are also studies that show the keto diet can largely help improve the HDL levels in your body.

This is due to reducing the consumption of carbohydrates and increasing the intake of healthy fats.

Helps Increase Patterns of LDL cholesterol

LDL cholesterol is commonly referred to and antagonized as the bad cholesterol and can increase the risk of cardiac disorders. There exists a misconception that an increase in LDL cholesterol levels holds the potential to increase your factors of risk for many kinds of cardiac disorders. That, however, is not true. The impact is determined by the size of the particles. As per studies, smaller particles result in greater risks of cardiac disorders.

People who have LDL cholesterol particles that are larger suffer from minimum risk of getting any kind of cardiac disorders. As a result, it is the size of the particles that can decide the factors of risk and their direct relevance to your health and your lifestyle as well.

But this raises the question – how is the keto diet instrumental in enlarging these particles?

Well, every question leads back to the same root of all problems – carbohydrates.

The sizes of these particles are directly linked to the amount of carbohydrates you tend to consume. The vaster the amount of carbs consumed, the smaller the size of these particles will become. When they keep getting smaller, the factors of risk of cardiac disorders will be increasing with each passing day. So, when you opt for a diet like the keto diet, what happens is that you are restricting your intake of carbs in all manners possible, and that also means helping your body deal with all the problems the vast amount of carbs have previously caused or were going to cause.

Thus, when you reduce your intake of carbs, you are nudging the size of these particles to increase and help decrease risk factors of cardiac disorders.

Other Health Benefits

Helps Strengthen Eyes

High levels of sugar can be very toxic and have damaging effects on your eyesight. It also increases your risk of cataracts. But when you follow a diet that has little next to no sugar in it, these risks are instantly eliminated.

Treats Gastrointestinal Issues

Acid reflux, irritable bowel syndrome, heartburn, gallstones and bloating are all problems related to digestion and they can leads to other serious problems if not put under control in time. One of the best methods to handle these issues is by making radical changes in your eating habits and overall diet. A diet that is low-carb directly deals with the origin of these issues. A keto diet helps you improve your eating habits and eases whatever pains you could be experiencing because of enteric problems.

Treats Brain Disorders

Traditionally, long before the keto diet started gaining any popularity for its wide array of benefits, it was actually used as a method to treat epilepsy in children who failed to respond to medication. To function, the brain requires carbohydrates, but thankfully it can also work with ketones, that are generated when the carbohydrates intake is drastically decreased.

Acne

Consuming vast amounts of carbohydrates is deleterious for your skin, and the near absolute absence of carbohydrates in the ketogenic diet automatically helps cleanse your skin. As a result, it improves the overall health of your skin and also makes it glow and evens it out. It is also helpful in reducing skin problems like lesions and inflammation.

Enhanced Mental Focus

As perplexing as it might sound to some, the keto diet can largely help strengthen your mental performance, as ketones are an essential energy source for the brain. They also enhance our focus and our brain's capacity to perform well.

Boosts Women's Health

The keto diet can help in strengthening and improving fertility. Its low-carb factor can also effectively help treat and control the hormonal disorders like PCOS (Polycystic Ovarian Syndrome) that some women face – in fact; the diet can also help in overcoming symptoms such as obesity, acne and irregular menstrual cycles.

Boosts Energy Levels

When carbohydrates turn into glucose and become the main source of energy for our bodies, they make us feel rather tired and fatigued. But fats are a much more feasible power source for the body, and they keep us from feeling lethargic. As they are quite fulfilling, they make sure we are sated and full for lengthy time periods.

Teeth and Gum Protection

When we consume less amounts of sugar, the pH level of the mouth remains normal and that prevents a specific kind of bacteria from breeding. The bacteria is behind gum infections and tooth decay. If you suffer from any kind of gum disease, being 3 months on the keto diet will help decrease it a lot.

Chapter Four: Dairy-free: What, Why, and How

What

People who decide to go for a dairy-free diet or choose to do a diet but without dairy (such dairy-free keto), they do it for their own set of reasons. Some do it to deal with health issues like bloating, digestion problems, skin issues, respiratory conditions and other things that stem from the consumption of dairy products.

As per studies, thirty million to fifty million Americans suffer from lactose intolerance. Thankfully, there exist enough plant based foods and other foodstuffs that are dairy-free to fulfill your body's nutritional needs.

Simply put – a dairy-free diet is a diet that is devoid of milk and any products made from it or have milk as one of their ingredients.

People who are intolerant towards lactose might opt for removing or reducing foods from their diet that contain any amount of lactose.

It might be possible for some to have small portions of food products that contain milk proteins; they might discover their digestive systems finds a fermented form of dairy easier to digest. Those with an allergy related to cow's milk based foods should absolutely remove milk proteins from their food intake and look for alternatives for food allergies that can provide them with calcium and other essential nutrients.

All prime sources of dairy you need to stay away from when going for a dairy-free diet are – milk, butter, cheese, cream, sour cream, cottage cheese, puddings, gelato, whey, casein, custards and sherbet.

Why

If you are wondering why exactly a dairy-free diet is beneficial for you, read on ahead about all the benefits:

Better Digestion

If estimations are anything to go by, of the entire world's population, around 75% has lactose intolerance to some degree. When you follow a diet that is dairy-free and make sure to stick to it, you can successfully avoid digestive symptoms, so many people suffer from on a daily basis.

Removing dairy from your diet can help relieve stomach pain, cramps, gas, bloating, nausea and diarrhea. Dairy has also been observed as key in triggering symptoms of Irritable Bowel Syndrome and other digestive problems.

Clears Your Skin

As per studies, the presence of anabolic steroids and growth hormones in milk add to milk's potential as a stimulant in the case of acne. When you dairy-free and also take some probiotic supplements, it can help in treating acne in a natural manner, without resolving to medications that are harsh on both your skin and health and come with a variety of side-effects.

Reduced Bloating

Dairy products are a common reason behind complaints of bloating among those who are sensitive to dairy or are allergic to it. On its own, bloating is generally an issue with digestion. For a lot of people, the reason behind excessive gas in their intestines, which is how bloating occurs, is because of insufficient digestion of protein – which is an inability of breaking down carbohydrates and sugars completely, and imbalances in gut related bacteria.

These factors are probably due to dairy sensitivities or allergic reactions to them. Following a dairy-free diet can be helpful in getting rid of a bloated tummy.

Reduces Oxidative Stress

It makes sense why diets that are rich in milk and milk-based products are promoted so rigorously. It is mostly to reduce the chances of osteoporotic fractures, which would, in turn, result in the reduction of health care costs.

As per research, consuming high amounts of milk could have unwanted effects, as milk is D-galactose's primary dietary source. D-galactose impacts the process of inflammation and oxidative stress.

According to evidence in several species of animals, a chronic form of exposure to D-galactose is harmful to health. In fact, a low dose of D-galactose triggers changes that are similar to natural aging processes in animals, along with a lifespan that has been shortened as a result of chronic inflammation, oxidative stress damage, decreased immune system, and neurodegeneration.

Reduced Risk of Cancer

As per some research, consumption of milk products can increase one's cancer developing risks. A calcium intake that is high, and mainly sourced from dairy products, can increase the risk of prostate cancer as it lowers a hormone's concentration, a hormone that is believed to protect us against prostate cancer.

There might also be contaminant like pesticides present in milk products, and these have been observed to encourage the cell growth of breast cancer.

A lot of people refuse to believe it, but cancer has a real link to our eating habits. And since it appears to alleviate the risk of some forms of cancer in specific people, opting for a dairy-free diet could help reduce the risks of some types of cancer.

Good for the Respiratory System

Consuming excess amounts of milk has been linked to asthma and increase mucus production in the respiratory tract. People with dairy sensitivities or allergies often report respiratory symptoms – staying away could help people with such problems.

Helps Milk Sensitivity and Allergy

There exists no true cure for being allergic to milk, except for avoiding it entirely along with other milk-based products. Digestive enzymes and probiotics can help people in digesting the proteins in milk a bit better but only in the case of their allergy not being severe. However, for the majority, removing dairy entirely from their diet is the only solution.

For those who are intolerant towards lactose, a lack of or reducing lactase could lead to unabsorbed lactose passing into the colon, which could lead to fermentation of bacteria which in turn would give rise to symptoms such as diarrhea, flatulence, nausea and bloating.

According to a lot of studies, such gastrointestinal symptoms are improved when the diet is entirely cleansed of milk.

Another allergy that is identified as an issue in infancy and could affect about 15% of infants is milk protein allergy. As per speculation, when the mother consumes milk protein, it is passed onto the infant during breastfeeding. Because of this, mothers are often recommended by mom to remove dairy from their diet if their infants show any negative reactions to breast milk.

Now that you have read about both the benefits of the keto diet, and the benefits of going dairy-free, don't you think the combined benefits turn both into a dynamic duo? If you think about all the way your health can attain its best by doing a dairy-free keto diet, wait until you reach the recipes section of this book. They are exactly what you need to get started on your dairy-free keto journey.

How

So far there does not exist any therapies suitable to treat allergies against cow's milk, other than removing it from your diet completely. As a result, being aware of dairy alternative is quite important.

The nutrients that we are at the risk of losing out on by eliminating dairy are calcium, magnesium, and potassium.

Goat Milk

It still is dairy, yes, but it is high in its content of fatty acids and is a lot easier to absorb and assimilate into the body as opposed to cow's milk. Goat milk has a lot concentration of lactose and the particles of fat in this milk are also smaller. As its casein levels are reduced, it becomes a better option for people who are sensitive to casein protein.

It might surprise you, but goat's milk is nutritionally just as high, as it has a high amount of calcium – it can supply thirty-three percent of your everyday value, along with that it is rich in vitamin B2, Vitamin A, potassium, phosphorus, and magnesium.

Coconut Milk

It is globally acclaimed as one of the best options when you go dairy-free. It's natural liquid present in mature coconuts. The milk is in the 'meat' of the coconut, which, when blended, gives us the thick coconut milk. It is 100% devoid of lactose, soy and dairy. Even though cow's milk offers more calcium as opposed to coconut milk, it can be made up for with foods that are rich in calcium, such as broccoli, kale, bok choy, etc.

However, it is worthy to note, coconut milk is high in fat and calories. Although the fat is of a healthier type, it is essential you are mindful of the portion especially if trying to lose weight.

Almond Milk

The nutritional aspects of almonds are many and just as essential. Not only are they rich with their content of unsaturated fatty acids, but also they are low in saturated fatty acids. They have filling fiber, protective and unique Phytosterols antioxidants, and also plant protein.

Almond milk also has probiotic components that can help with detoxification, digestions, and healthy growth of bacteria in the gut flora that is vital in the utilization of nutrients sourced from food and prevents nutritional deficiencies.

Chapter Five: The Dos and Don'ts of Food on Keto

Every diet you will ever come across will have an elaborate list of what you can or cannot eat while on the diet. That is kind of the whole point of a diet.

Anyway, the ketogenic diet is no different. It too has some dos and don'ts. But one of the best aspects is how the section of what's allowed is always greater than what is restricted. If you truly want to benefit from the keto diet and all the amazing impacts it can have on your life, try to stick to these dos and don'ts for the best results.

What to Eat
Meat, fatty fish, eggs:

The keto diet is a diet that is rich in meat content. It allows you to consume a vast variety of meats such as – ham, steak, turn, bacon, chicken, red meat, sausage, etc. Other than that, you are also allowed to consume fish that are high in natural fats. It is advisable to opt for trout, tuna, mackerel, salmon, etc. You can also consume eggs but make sure they are pastured eggs as they are rich in omega-3 and it is a component that can benefit you when you are on the keto diet.

Vegetables that have low carb content:

Opt for vegetables like tomatoes, peppers, onions, lettuce, broccoli, spinach, chives, celery stalk, endive, bamboo shoots, chard, radishes, bok choy, zucchini, cucumber, asparagus, etc. Try to avoid vegetables that are starchy, such as potatoes, sweet potatoes, etc.

Fruits:

Avocado, and for occasional consumption – mulberries, strawberries, blueberries, raspberries, olives, cranberries, and coconut.

Nuts and Seeds:

Pumpkin seeds, flaxseeds, almonds, walnuts, chia seeds, pecans, hazelnuts, sesame seeds, macadamia nuts, etc. are allowed.

(If you are NOT doing a dairy-free keto)

Cream, cheese, and butter:

Grass-fed butter, cheese but the unprocessed varieties – goat cheese, blue cheese, cheddar cheese, cream cheese and mozzarella cheese, etc.

Condiments:

Pepper, herbs, salt, pesto, mayonnaise, lemon or lime zest and juice, and other spices, etc.

Beverages:

Tea – herbal or black, coffee – black or with coconut milk, etc. If you are using dairy, you can add cream to your coffee.

Healthy Oils:

During the keto diet, it is essential to opt for oils that are healthy and help amplify the effects of the diet. You can go for – extra-virgin olive oil, avocado oil and coconut oil, etc.

Chapter Six: Dairy-free Ketogenic Breakfast Recipes

Celery Root Rosti (Hash Browns)

Serves: 3-4

Ingredients:

- 3-4 celery roots, peeled, grated
- Salt to taste
- Pepper to taste
- 2 tablespoons coconut oil

Serving options (optional): Use any

- Tomato salsa
- Scrambled eggs
- Roasted vegetables

Method:

1. Sprinkle salt and pepper over the celery root.
2. Place a pan over medium high heat. Add oil. When the oil melts, add celery root. Spread it all over the pan to make one large one or else make smaller sized hash browns. Smaller sized ones can be cooked in batches.
3. Cook until underside is cooked and golden brown.
4. Flip sides and cook the other side too.
5. Chop into wedges.
6. Serve with any of the suggested options or any other keto friendly, dairy-free options of your choice.

Breakfast Biscuit

Serves: 2

Ingredients:

- 2 tablespoons coconut flour
- A pinch sea salt
- 2 teaspoons coconut oil
- ¼ cup golden flaxseed meal
- 1 teaspoon aluminum-free baking powder
- 2 large eggs, beaten

Method:

1. Add all the dry ingredients into a bowl.
2. Add coconut oil and mix well until crumbly in texture. Add egg and mix well.
3. Grease 2 small ovenproof bowls or ramekins and add the mixture into the bowls.
4. Bake in a preheated oven at 350° F for about 15 minutes or until firm.
5. Alternately, you can microwave it on high for about 55 seconds.
6. When done, cool on a cooling rack.
7. Serve.

Spinach Omelet with Egg whites

Serves: 2

Ingredients:

- 2 yolks
- 10 egg whites
- 1 tomato, chopped
- 1 medium onion, chopped
- 1 cup spinach, shredded
- A handful basil, chopped
- 2 cloves garlic, minced
- ¼ cup almond milk
- Cooking spray

Method:

1. Whisk together yolks, whites, along with almond milk in a bowl.
2. Take a nonstick pan and place it over medium heat. Spray with cooking spray. When oil is heated, add onion, tomato and spinach and sauté for a couple of minutes.
3. Remove the vegetables and place on a plate.
4. Spray the pan again with cooking spray. Let the pan heat.
5. Lower heat and pour half the egg mixture into the pan. When the eggs are set, place half the vegetable mixture on one half of the omelet. Fold the other half over the filling.
6. Remove on to a serving plate and serve.

7. Repeat the above 2 steps with the remaining egg mixture and vegetables to make the other omelet.

Classic Bacon and Eggs

Serves: 2

Ingredients:

- 4 eggs
- 2 ¾ ounces bacon slices
- A handful fresh parsley, chopped
- 4 cherry tomatoes, halved
- Salt to taste
- Pepper to taste

Method:

1. Place a skillet over medium heat. Add bacon and cook until crisp.
2. Remove the bacon from the skillet on some paper towels. When cool enough to handle, chop or break into smaller pieces.
3. Cook eggs with the fat in the skillet, as per your preference.
4. Place eggs and bacon on serving plates. Sprinkle salt and pepper on top and serve.

Coconut Porridge

Serves: 2

Ingredients:

- 2 ounces coconut oil
- 2 tablespoons coconut flour
- 8 tablespoons coconut cream
- 2 eggs
- ½ teaspoon ground psyllium husk powder
- A pinch salt

Method:

1. Add all the ingredients into a nonstick pan and stir.
2. Place the pan over low heat, stirring all the time until you get the desired texture.
3. Garnish with frozen berries and coconut milk or cream if desired and serve.

Fat Bomb Smoothie

Serves: 2

Ingredients:

- 2 cups coconut milk
- 2 tablespoon peanut butter
- 1 teaspoon ground cinnamon
- 4 tablespoons coconut oil
- 1 teaspoon vanilla extract
- Ice cubes, as required

Method:

1. Add coconut milk, peanut butter, cinnamon, coconut oil, vanilla and ice into a blender and blend until smooth.
2. Pour into glasses and serve.
3. For a change in taste, you can add keto friendly non-dairy chocolate protein powder or add a few slices avocado while blending.

Blueberry Smoothie

Serves: 1

Ingredients:

- 1 cup coconut milk
- ½ tablespoon lemon juice
- ¼ cup blueberries, fresh or frozen
- ¼ teaspoon vanilla extract

Method:

1. Add all the ingredients into a blender and blend until smooth.
2. Pour into a tall glass and serve with crushed ice.

Chapter Seven: Dairy-free Ketogenic Snack Recipes

Salty Chocolate Treat

Serves: 5

Ingredients:

- 1 ¾ ounces dairy-free dark chocolate
- 1 tablespoon coconut chips, unsweetened, roasted
- A large pinch flaky salt or to taste
- 5 hazelnuts or pecans or walnuts
- ½ tablespoon pumpkin seeds

Method:

1. Set a double boiler. Add chocolate into a heatproof bowl and place on the double boiler. Stir frequently until chocolate melts.
2. Pour melted chocolate into 5 cupcake liners.
3. Sprinkle nuts, chocolate chips and seeds into the liners.
4. Sprinkle salt op top.
5. Cool completely and refrigerate until use.

Seed Crackers

Serves: 15

Ingredients:

- ¼ cup almond flour
- ¾ teaspoon sea salt
- ¼ cup sesame seeds
- ¼ cup sunflower seeds
- ¼ cup flaxseeds or chia seeds
- ¼ teaspoon pumpkin seeds
- ½ tablespoon psyllium husk powder
- 2 tablespoons coconut oil, melted
- ½ cup boiling water

Method:

1. Mix together almond flour, salt, all the seeds and psyllium husk powder into a bowl. Pour water into the bowl. Form into dough.
2. Line a baking sheet with parchment paper.
3. Place the dough at the center of the paper. Cover with another paper and roll the dough until it is about ½ inch thick.
4. After rolling, cut the dough with a knife into squares.
5. Place the baking sheet in a preheated oven at 350 ° F for about 10-15 minutes until golden brown. Cool and separate the squares.
6. Store in an airtight container.

Zucchini Chips with Smoked Paprika

Serves: 4

Ingredients:

- 2 medium zucchinis
- 1 teaspoon salt or to taste
- 4 tablespoons olive oil
- 2 teaspoons smoked paprika
- ½ teaspoon pepper powder to taste

Method:

1. Cut the zucchini into ¼ inch thick slices, crosswise with a mandolin slicer or a knife.
2. Place the zucchini in a colander in layers sprinkled with salt and pepper. Set aside for an hour.
3. Pat dry the zucchini slices with a paper towel and place on a baking tray that is lined with parchment paper. Brush the parchment paper with oil.
4. Brush the top of the slices with oil. Sprinkle paprika and pepper.
5. Bake in a preheated oven at 250° F for 45 minutes. Turn off the oven and let the chips remain inside for an hour.
6. Cool completely.
7. Transfer into airtight container.

Zesty Nacho Kale Chips

Serves: 4-6

Ingredients:

- 4 large bunch kale, discard stems and hard ribs, torn into bite size pieces
- 1 cup tahini
- ½ cup nutritional yeast
- 1 large red bell pepper, chopped
- 2 tablespoons golden balsamic vinegar (optional)
- 2 teaspoons garlic powder
- 1 teaspoon pepper powder or to taste
- 1 cup sunflower seed butter
- 1 cup apple cider vinegar
- ½ cup lemon juice or to taste
- 4 tablespoons sesame oil or olive oil
- 2-3 drops stevia (optional)
- 1 tablespoon coconut aminos or tamari
- 1 teaspoon onion powder
- 1 teaspoon salt or to taste
- Cooking spray

Method:

1. Sprinkle salt on the kale. Spray with cooking spray. Keep it aside for a while.
2. Spread the leaves on a greased baking sheet.
3. Bake in a preheated oven at 250° F until crisp. It may take a couple of hours.

4. Meanwhile, add rest of the ingredients into a blender and blend until smooth.
5. Pour sauce into a large bowl.
6. When the chips are ready, add chips into the bowl of sauce. Toss with tongs and serve right away.
7. If you are not using all the chips and sauce, store in separate airtight containers. Refrigerate the sauce until use. Remove from the refrigerator 40-50 minutes before serving. Add kale chips, toss and serve.

Broccoli Tots

Makes: 40-50

Ingredients:

- 4 medium heads broccoli, cut into florets
- 1 cup yellow bell pepper, finely chopped
- 1 cup almond meal
- Salt to taste
- Freshly ground pepper to taste
- 1 cup onion, finely chopped
- 2 egg whites
- 2 eggs
- A handful fresh parsley, chopped
- Cooking spray

Method:

1. Spray a baking sheet with cooking spray.
2. Place a large pot, half filled with water over medium high heat.
3. When the water begins to boil, add salt and broccoli. Cook for 4-5 minutes or until tender.
4. Drain and transfer into the food processor bowl. Pulse until very fine.
5. Squeeze out as much as moisture as possible from the broccoli and add into a bowl.
6. Add rest of the ingredients and mix well.
7. Shape into tots using about 1-2 tablespoons of the mixture.
8. Place on the prepared baking sheet.

9. Bake in a preheated oven at 375° F until crisp.
10. Serve with a keto friendly dip of your choice.

Avocado Hummus

Serves: 5-6

Ingredients:

- 2 ripe avocados, peeled, pitted, roughly chopped
- A large handful fresh cilantro, chopped
- 2 tablespoons lemon juice
- 3 tablespoons sunflower seeds
- 3 tablespoons olive oil
- 5 teaspoons tahini paste
- ½ teaspoon ground cumin
- 1 small clove garlic, peeled,
- Salt to taste
- Pepper to taste
- Water, if required

Method:

1. Add all the ingredients into a blender and blend until smooth. Add water if the hummus is very thick. Blend again.
2. Transfer into a bowl. Taste and adjust the seasoning and oil if required.
3. Serve.
4. Serving options: With keto friendly crackers, cucumber sticks, in wraps, as a side dish, etc.

Chapter Eight: Dairy-free Keto Side Dish Recipes

Rutabaga Curls

Serves: 2

Ingredients:

- ¾ pound rutabaga
- ½ tablespoon paprika or chili powder
- 6-7 teaspoons olive oil
- ½ teaspoon salt

Method:

1. Make noodles of the rutabaga using a spiralizer. You can also make noodles using a julienne peeler or with a sharp knife. Cut into bite size pieces.
2. Add the noodles into a bowl. Add rest of the ingredients and toss well.
3. Transfer on to a baking sheet. Spread it evenly.
4. Bake in a preheated oven at 450° F for about 10 minutes.
5. Serve right away.

Coleslaw

Serves: 8

Ingredients:

- 1 medium green cabbage, thinly sliced
- 2 teaspoons salt
- ¼ teaspoon fennel seeds (optional)
- 2 tablespoons Dijon mustard
- Juice of a lemon
- ¾ cup mayonnaise or to taste
- Pepper to taste

Method:

1. Add cabbage into a colander. Add salt and lemon juice and mix well.
2. Let it sit in the colander for 10 minutes.
3. Add cabbage back into the bowl. Add rest of the ingredients. Mix well.
4. Serve.

Roasted Radishes with Rosemary

Serves: 4

Ingredients:

- 6 cups radishes, quartered if large in size else halved, chop the leaves and keep aside
- 1 teaspoons sea salt or to taste
- 15 whole black peppercorns
- 6 sprigs fresh rosemary, chopped
- 6 tablespoon olive oil

Method:

1. Add salt and peppercorns into a mortar and pestle and crush the peppercorns.
2. Place together in a bowl, radishes, 4 tablespoons oil, rosemary and the crushed pepper. Toss well.
3. Transfer on to a greased baking sheet. Spread it in a single layer.
4. Roast in a preheated oven at 425° F until crisp and brown.
5. Meanwhile, place a skillet over medium heat. Add the remaining oil. When the oil is heated, add the radish leaves, a little salt and sauté until the leaves are wilted.
6. Add the roasted radish and stir well.
7. Serve right away.

Roasted Fennel with Lemon and Sugar snaps

Serves: 2

Ingredients:

- Juice of ½ lemon
- 1 ½ tablespoons olive oil
- 1 tablespoon sunflower seeds or pumpkin seeds, roasted
- ½ pound fresh fennel, chopped into wedges
- 2 ¾ ounces sugar snaps, shredded
- Pepper to taste
- Salt to taste

Method:

1. Place fennel in a baking dish. Pour oil over it. Toss well. Sprinkle salt and pepper and toss well.
2. Squeeze the juice from the lemon and use in some other recipe. Cut the lemon rind into 3-4 pieces and place it in the baking dish, all around the fennel pieces.
3. Roast in a preheated oven at 450° F for 20-30 minutes or until golden brown in color.
4. Add sugar snap peas and pumpkin seeds and mix well.
5. Goes well as a side with chicken, fish, lamb, pork, turkey or beef.

Fried Green Cabbage

Serves: 2

Ingredients:

- ¾ pound green cabbage, shredded
- Salt to taste
- Pepper to taste
- 1 ½ ounces coconut oil

Method:

1. Place a skillet over medium heat. Add oil. When oil melts, add cabbage and sauté until the cabbage is cooked as per your desire. Lower heat halfway through cooking. Stir frequently.
2. Add salt and pepper and mix well.
3. Serve hot.

Celery Root and Cauliflower Puree with Garlicky Greens

Serves: 2-3

Ingredients:

For celery root and cauliflower puree:

- 1 celery root of about 8 ounces, peeled, cut into cubes of ½ inch each
- ¼ teaspoon salt
- 8 ounces cauliflower, cut into small florets
- 1 ½ tablespoons extra -virgin olive oil

For sautéed chard:

- 1 bunch Swiss chard, rinsed, cut leaves into strips and thinly cut the stems up to ¾ the stems
- 1 small clove garlic, minced
- Sea salt to taste
- ½ tablespoon extra-virgin olive oil
- A pinch red pepper flakes

Method:

1. To make celery root and cauliflower puree: Steam the celery roots and cauliflower in the steaming equipment you have. Steam until tender.
2. Place the steamed vegetables into a food processor. Add a couple of tablespoons of the

cooked liquid, salt and oil. Blend until the texture you desire is achieved.

3. Cover and keep warm.
4. To make sautéed chard: Place a skillet over medium heat. Add oil. When the oil is heated, add garlic and red pepper flakes and sauté for a few seconds until fragrant.
5. Add chard leaves and stems and sauté for 2-3 minutes.
6. Cover and cook for some more time until tender. Add salt and stir.
7. Serve celery root and cauliflower puree over the sautéed chard.

Cauliflower Rice

Serves: 2-3

Ingredients:

- ¾ pound cauliflower, chopped into florets
- 1 onion, finely diced (optional)
- 4 tablespoons olive oil or coconut oil
- 4 cloves garlic, minced (optional)
- ¼ teaspoon turmeric powder (optional)
- Salt to taste
- Pepper powder to taste

Method:

1. Add the cauliflower florets into the food processor and pulse until you get a rice like texture. You can also grate the cauliflower.
2. Place a large nonstick skillet over medium high heat. Add oil. When the oil is heated, add onions and sauté until translucent. Add garlic and sauté until fragrant. Add turmeric powder and sauté for 5-8 seconds.
3. Add cauliflower rice and sauté for about 5-6 minutes. Remove from heat.
4. Sprinkle salt and pepper just before serving.
5. If you are not using the optional ingredients, you can also cook in the microwave by adding cauliflower rice into a microwave safe bowl. Cover the bowl with plastic wrap. Microwave on high for 5-6 minutes.

6. Unwrap and add oil and salt. Mix well and serve.

Roasted Tomato Salad

Serves: 2-3

Ingredients:

- ¾ pound cherry tomatoes
- ½ teaspoon sea salt
- 1 scallion, sliced
- 1 ½ tablespoons olive oil
- ¼ teaspoon pepper
- ½ tablespoon red wine vinegar

Method:

1. Pour oil on the cherry tomatoes and toss well. Add salt and pepper and toss well.
2. Grill or roast in an oven until the tomatoes begin to get soft and charred.
3. Transfer on to a plate. Place scallions on top. Drizzle vinegar and some more oil if desired and serve.

Celeriac "Grits"

Serves: 4

Ingredients:

- 4 medium celeriac's, trim the outer brown layer, cubed
- 2 tablespoons pure avocado oil
- 1 teaspoon pepper powder
- 4 cups chicken stock
- 2 medium onion, chopped
- 2 teaspoons sea salt or to taste
- 4 cloves garlic, minced

Method:

1. Add the celeriac to the food processor and pulse until you get corn grit like texture. You can also grate the cauliflower.
2. Place a large nonstick skillet over medium high heat. Add oil. When the oil is heated, add onions and sauté until translucent. Add garlic and sauté until fragrant.
3. Add rest of the ingredients into the skillet and stir.
4. Cover and cook for 10-12 minutes. Uncover and cook until most of the liquid is absorbed.
5. Serve hot.

Chapter Nine: Dairy-free Ketogenic Main Course Recipes

Cream of Chicken Soup

Serves: 4

Ingredients:

- 2 medium cauliflowers, broken into florets
- 2 cups chicken broth
- 1 teaspoon sea salt
- Freshly ground pepper to taste
- ¼ teaspoon dried thyme
- ½ cup chicken thighs, cooked, finely chopped
- 1 1/3 cups almond milk, unsweetened
- 2 teaspoons onion powder
- ½ teaspoon garlic powder
- ¼ teaspoon celery seeds (optional)
- ½ cup Collagen protein beef gelatin (optional)

Method:

1. Set aside the chicken and gelatin and add rest of the ingredients into a soup pot.
2. Place the soup pot over medium heat. Cover with a lid and let it boil.
3. Lower heat when it begins to boil. Simmer until cauliflower is soft.

4. Turn off the heat. Take out about a cup of the cooked liquid and add into a bowl.
5. Add a teaspoon of gelatin at a time into the bowl of cooked liquid. Whisk well each time until the gelatin is dissolved. Continue doing this until the entire gelatin is added.
6. Pour the gelatin mixture into a blender. Also, add the cooked cauliflower mixture.
7. Blend until smooth and creamy.
8. Pour the soup back into the pot. Place the pot over low heat.
9. Add chicken and stir. Cover and cook until the soup is heated thoroughly.
10. Ladle into soup bowls and serve.

Cabbage Soup with Chicken Quenelles

Serves: 8

Ingredients:

- 2 pounds ground chicken
- 2 tablespoons dried parsley
- 1 teaspoon salt
- 2 chicken cubes
- 2 pounds green cabbage or savoy cabbage
- Salt to taste
- Pepper to taste
- 2 eggs
- 2 teaspoons onion powder
- ½ teaspoon ground nutmeg
- 8 cups water
- 4 ounces coconut oil
- 2 chicken bouillon cubes

For parsley butter:

- 10 ounces coconut oil, at room temperature
- Salt to taste
- Pepper to taste
- 2 tablespoons fresh parsley, minced

Method:

1. Add parsley, coconut oil, salt and pepper into a bowl. Mix well.
2. To make quenelles: Add chicken, salt, pepper, garlic powder, onion powder and eggs into a bowl and mix well.

58

3. Chill for 15-20 minutes in the refrigerator.
4. Make small balls of the mixture of about 2.5 cm diameter.
5. Place a soup pot over medium high heat. Add coconut oil. When the coconut oil melts, add cabbage and sauté until light golden brown.
6. Add chicken bouillon cubes and water and stir. When it begins to boil, lower heat.
7. Drop the quenelles, one at a time into the simmering broth. Let it simmer for 10-15 minutes or until the quenelle are cooked.
8. Ladle into soup bowls. Top with a blob of parsley butter and serve.

Thai Chicken Skillet

Serves: 6

Ingredients:

- 3 tablespoons coconut oil
- 1 ½ cups chicken stock
- 6 large bone-in chicken thighs trimmed of excess fat and skin
- ½ cup onion, chopped
- 3 cloves garlic, minced
- 9 ounces green bell pepper, chopped
- 3 tablespoons lime juice
- 1 ½ cups coconut milk
- Salt to taste
- Pepper to taste
- 2 tablespoons Thai curry paste or more to taste
- Cauliflower rice to serve

Toppings: Optional

- Handful fresh cilantro, chopped
- Lime juice
- Red chili pepper, sliced

Method:

1. Place a large skillet over high heat. Add 1-½ tablespoons of oil. When oil melts, place chicken with its skin side down, in a single layer.

2. Lower heat to medium high heat and cook for 5 minutes. Flip sides and cook for 3 minutes.
3. Remove chicken with a slotted spoon and place on a plate.
4. Add remaining oil into the skillet. Add onion and garlic and sauté until translucent.
5. Add bell pepper and sauté for a minute. Add remaining ingredients and mix well.
6. Add the chicken back into the skillet with the skin side up. Cook for 10-12 minutes.
7. Transfer into a preheated oven. Broil for a few minutes until crisp. Top with optional toppings if desired.
8. Serve with cauliflower rice on the side.

Low Carb Chicken and Vegetable Curry

Serves: 8

Ingredients:

- 2 pounds chicken thighs, boneless, chopped into bite sized pieces if desired
- 2 yellow onions, chopped
- 16 ounces broccoli, cut into smaller florets
- 2 red chili peppers, deseeded, chopped
- 7 ounces fresh green beans, chopped
- 6 tablespoons coconut oil
- 3 ½ cans (14.5 ounces each) coconut milk or coconut cream
- 2 tablespoons red curry paste or to taste
- 2 tablespoons fresh ginger, grated
- ½ teaspoon cayenne pepper or to taste (optional)
- Salt to taste
- Cauliflower rice to serve

Method:

1. Add oil into a Dutch oven or a large saucepan.
2. Add onion, ginger and chili pepper and sauté until onions turn translucent.
3. Stir in the curry paste and chicken. Mix well.
4. Cook until light brown. Add more oil if required.

5. Add vegetables and the thick part of coconut cream and milk. Use the liquid in some other recipe. Cook until done.
6. Serve hot over cauliflower rice.

Italian Meatza

Serves: 8

For the crust:

- 2 pounds lean ground beef
- 2 tablespoons fresh basil chopped or 2 teaspoons dried basil
- 4 tablespoons mixed dried Italian herbs like oregano, thyme, parsley, etc.
- 1 teaspoon salt
- 1 teaspoon black pepper
- 2 cloves garlic, minced
- Fresh basil, chopped to garnish

For topping: Use any, as required (optional)

- 1 cup tomato sauce
- ½ cup sundried tomatoes, sliced
- 1 red bell pepper, sliced
- 10 olives, sliced
- 1 artichoke hearts (canned or packed in oil), chopped
- 1 cup arugula leaves

Method:

1. To make meat crust: Mix together all the ingredients of crust in a bowl.
2. Add the mixture to a large pie pan or into 2 smaller pie pans. Press it well on to the bottom of the pan.

3. Bake in a preheated oven at 400° F for about 15-18 minutes. Drain off the fat that is remaining in the pan.
4. For topping: Spread tomato sauce over the baked beef crusts.
5. Sprinkle toppings and bake for about 8-10 minutes.
6. Cut into wedges and serve.

Steak and Broccoli Stir Fry

Serves: 4

Ingredients:

- 8 ounces coconut oil
- 18 ounces broccoli, chop the florets as well as the stems
- 2 tablespoons tamari sauce (optional)
- Salt to taste
- Pepper to taste
- 1 ½ pounds rib eye steaks, sliced
- 2 yellow onion, sliced
- 2 tablespoons pumpkin seeds

Method:

1. Place a wok or frying pan over medium heat. Add half the oil. When it melts, add steak slices and cook until brown. Sprinkle salt and pepper. Mix well.
2. Remove steaks with a slotted spoon and place on a plate.
3. Add broccoli and onions into the pan. Sauté until broccoli is crisp as well as tender. Add more coconut oil if needed.
4. Add tamari and mix well. Add steak back into the pan and mix well. Taste and adjust the seasonings if necessary.
5. Serve right away with pumpkin seeds.

Pork and Green Pepper Stir Fry

Serves: 4

Ingredients:

- 1 1/3 pound pork shoulder slices
- 4 scallions, sliced
- 4 tablespoons almonds
- Salt to taste
- Pepper to taste
- 4 green bell peppers, sliced
- 8 ounces coconut oil or lard
- 2 teaspoons chili paste

Method:

1. Place a wok or frying pan over medium heat. Add most of the oil.
2. When it melts, add pork and raise the heat to high heat. Cook until brown.
3. Add scallions and bell peppers. Stir and add chili paste. Mix well. Sauté until slightly tender.
4. Add salt and pepper and mix well.
5. Top with almonds and remaining oil and serve right away.

Spicy Pulled Pork

Serves: 3

Ingredients:

- 1 pound pork shoulder
- ½ tablespoon cocoa nibs or cocoa powder
- ¼ teaspoon ground ginger
- ¼ teaspoon anise seeds or fennel seeds
- ¼ tablespoon black pepper powder
- ¼ teaspoon cayenne pepper
- ½ tablespoon salt
- 1 tablespoon olive oil

Method:

1. Add all the spices and cocoa nibs into a grinder and process until fine. You can also pound using a mortar and pestle.
2. Rub this mixture all over the pork. Place in a baking dish or rimmed baking sheet.
3. Bake in a preheated oven at 400° F for a few hours until tender.
4. Alternately, you can cook in a slow cooker.
5. When the pork is done, remove the pork and set aside on your cutting board.
6. When cool enough to handle, shred with a pair of forks.
7. Serve with roasted tomato salad and avocado hummus.

Ground Pork Tacos

Serves: 6 (5 wraps per serving)

Ingredients:

- 2 pounds ground pork
- 1 ½ teaspoons onion powder
- 1 teaspoon ground cumin
- 20 large lettuce leaves or more if required
- 1 ½ teaspoons garlic powder
- 1 teaspoon sea salt
- ½ teaspoon ground pepper or to taste

For toppings:

- ¼ cup salsa
- 2 medium onions, chopped
- ¾ cup green bell pepper, chopped
- ¾ cup red bell pepper, chopped
- Or any other dairy-free keto toppings of your choice

Method:

1. Add pork, garlic powder, onion powder, salt, cumin, and pepper into a bowl. Mix well using your hands.
2. Place the skillet over medium heat. Add the meat mixture. Stir constantly and cook until brown.
3. Remove the pork with a slotted spoon and place in a bowl. Discard the fat that is remaining in the skillet.

4. Add salsa and mix well. Taste and adjust the seasonings if necessary.
5. Lay the lettuce leaves on your working area. Place some pork filling at the center.
6. Sprinkle peppers, and onions. Wrap and serve.

Creamy Cauliflower and Ground Beef Skillet

Serves: 2

Ingredients:

- 1 tablespoon coconut oil
- 1 clove garlic, chopped
- ½ pound lean ground beef
- Freshly cracked pepper to taste
- ¼ cup keto friendly mayonnaise + 2 tablespoons extra to top
- 2 tablespoons toasted sunflower seed butter
- ½ teaspoon fish sauce
- 2 large eggs
- ¼ ripe avocado, peeled, diced
- ½ tablespoon apple cider vinegar
- 2 tablespoons chopped onions
- 2 jalapeños peppers, sliced, divided
- ½ teaspoon Himalayan salt
- ½ pound grated cauliflower
- ¼ cup water
- ½ tablespoon coconut aminos
- ½ teaspoon ground cumin
- A handful fresh parsley, chopped

Method:

1. Place a cast iron skillet or a heavy bottomed skillet over medium high heat.

2. Add coconut oil. When the oil melts, add onion, garlic and half the jalapeño pepper and sauté for a few minutes until slightly soft.
3. Stir in beef, pepper and salt and cook until brown.
4. Reduce heat to medium low and add cauliflower and sauté for a couple of minutes.
5. Add mayonnaise, sun butter, water, coconut aminos, and cumin and fish sauce into a small bowl and whisk well. Pour into the skillet and mix well. Sauté for a few minutes until the mixture is slightly dry.
6. Turn off the heat. Make 2 cavities (big enough for an egg to fit in) in the mixture. Crack an egg into each of the cavity. Season with salt and pepper. Sprinkle the remaining jalapeños pepper slices over it.
7. Transfer the skillet into a preheated oven. Broil for 8-10 minutes until the eggs are cooked as per your liking.
8. Meanwhile, mix together in a bowl, 2 tablespoons mayonnaise and apple cider vinegar. Drizzle over the skillet.
9. Top with avocado and parsley. Pierce the egg yolks and serve.

Pan Grilled Lamb Chops and Cardoons

Serves: 4

Ingredients:

<u>For lamb chops:</u>

- 4 lamb shoulder chops
- 2 sprigs fresh rosemary
- Sea salt to taste
- 6 tablespoons olive oil
- 4 cloves garlic

<u>For cardoons:</u>

- Pepper powder to taste
- Sea salt to taste
- 2 bunches cardoons
-

Method:

1. To make lamb chops: Add garlic, rosemary, oil and salt into a small blender and blend until smooth. Alternately, you can pound in a mortar and pestle.
2. Transfer the mixture into a bowl.
3. Rub the mixture all over the lamb chops and place it in a bowl. Cover and set aside for at least 30 -60 minutes.
4. Place a cast iron skillet over medium heat. Place lamb chops on it. Cook in batches if your skillet is not large enough.

5. Cook for about 5 minutes or until brown. Flip sides and cook the other side too. The internal temperature with a cooking thermometer should register 125° F when the meat is cooked.
6. Remove from the pan and keep warm. Let the juices remain in the skillet.
7. To make cardoons: Rinse the cardoon stems. Using a sharp knife, peel off the outer most layer of the cardoon. Chop into 4 inch pieces.
8. Place a pot of water over medium heat. Add salt and cardoons. Cook until cardoons are tender. Drain.
9. Place the skillet back over heat. Add cardoons to it. Cook cardoons in the juice for a few minutes.
10. Serve cardoons with lamb chops.

Lamb Chops with Lemony Gremolata

Serves: 4

Ingredients:

For Gremolata:

- Zest of 1 lemon, grated
- ½ cup parsley leaves, loosely packed, minced
- 1 clove garlic, minced or pressed

For lamb chops:

- 1 tablespoon olive oil
- 1 tablespoon Gremolata
- ½ rack of lamb, cut into 4 individual rib chops
- Juice of ½ lemon
- Salt to taste
- Pepper to taste
- 1 tablespoon avocado oil

Method:

1. To make Gremolata: Mix together parsley, lemon zest and garlic on your cutting board. Mince the entire ingredients together a few times. Use 1 tablespoon of the Gremolata to make the lamb chops.
2. Add olive oil, 1 tablespoon Gremolata, lemon juice, salt and pepper into a bowl and mix well. Cover and chill for 1-4 hours. Stir a couple of times while it is marinating.
3. Remove from the refrigerator for 30-40 minutes before cooking.

4. Place a skillet over medium heat. Add oil. When the oil is heated, add chops and cook for about 3 minutes on each side for medium rare.
5. Sprinkle remaining Gremolata on top and serve.

Herb-Crusted Lamb Chops Recipe

Serves: 4

Ingredients:

- 4 large cloves garlic, smashed
- 2 sprigs fresh rosemary, snipped
- 2 tablespoons extra-virgin olive oil
- 2 sprigs fresh thyme, snipped
- 8 lamb loin chops (4 ½ inches)

Method:

1. Add garlic, herbs and half the oil into a bowl. Mix well. Add lamb chops and dredge the chops in the mixture.
2. Chill for 30-45 minutes.
3. Place an ovenproof skillet over high heat. Add remaining oil. When the oil is heated, add lamb chops and cook until brown on both the sides. It should take around 3 minutes on each side. Turn off the heat and transfer into a preheated oven
4. Bake at 400° F for about 10 minutes for medium rare.
5. When done, let it sit for 5 minutes.
6. Serve.

Thai Fish with Curry and Coconut

Serves: 2

Ingredients:

- ¾ pound fish fillets, cut crosswise into 1 inch slices
- ½ pound broccoli, cut into florets
- 1-2 tablespoons Thai red or green curry paste
- 7 ounces thick coconut milk or coconut cream
- 2 tablespoons coconut oil
- Sea salt to taste
- Pepper powder to taste
- ¼ cup fresh cilantro, chopped
- Cooking spray

Method:

1. Place fish in a baking dish. Place blobs of coconut oil over the fish at different places.
2. Add coconut milk, cilantro and red curry paste into a bowl and whisk well. Pepper. Pour over the fish.
3. Bake in a preheated oven at 400° F for about 20 minutes or until tender.
4. Meanwhile, steam the broccoli in salted water. Drain and set aside.
5. Serve fish curry with steamed broccoli.

Lemon Garlic Shrimp

Serves: 4

Ingredients:

- 20 large shrimp, peeled, deveined
- Juice of 2 lemons
- 6 cloves garlic, minced
- 1 teaspoon + 2 tablespoons sea salt
- A handful fresh parsley + extra to garnish
- 4 tablespoons 100% pure avocado oil
- 1 teaspoon smoked paprika
- ½ teaspoon + ½ teaspoon pepper powder
- Lemon wedges to serve

Method:

1. Add lemon juice, garlic, avocado oil, paprika, 1 teaspoon salt, paprika, parsley and ½ teaspoon pepper into a bowl. Mix well. Cover and set aside for a while for the flavors to set in.
2. Place a large pot of water with remaining salt over medium heat. Add remaining pepper and stir. Bring to the boil.
3. Add shrimp and simmer until shrimp turns pink. Turn off heat.
4. Drain and add shrimp into the lemon – oil mixture. Cover with foil and set aside for 10 minutes.

5. Serve shrimp over celeriac grits. Garnish with parsley and drizzle some lemon juice on top and serve.

Fish with Vegetables Baked in Foil

Serves: 8

Ingredients:

- 4 pounds white fish fillets, cut into bite size pieces
- 2 yellow onions, chopped
- 4 red bell peppers, sliced
- 2 fresh fennel or pointed cabbage or savoy cabbage, sliced
- 1 cup olives, pitted
- 2 limes, sliced
- 1 cup white wine
- 11 ounces coconut oil
- 1 leek, sliced
- 4 cloves garlic, sliced
- 24 cherry tomatoes, halved
- 2 carrots, peeled, sliced
- 1 cup fresh thyme or fresh parsley, chopped
- Salt to taste
- Pepper to taste
- 6 tablespoons olive oil

For quick aioli:

- 2 cups keto friendly, dairy-free mayonnaise
- Salt to taste
- Pepper to taste
- 2 cloves garlic, minced

Method:

1. Place a large sheet of parchment paper or foil in a roasting pan in such a way that it is hanging out from the pan. You should be able to make a packet in the end.
2. Place the fish in the roasting pan. Spread all the vegetables over the fish, evenly. Sprinkle garlic, salt, lime slices, olives, tomatoes and parsley.
3. Pour oil and dry white wine over it. Dot with coconut oil at different spots on the vegetables.
4. Fold the hanging foil over the filling. Seal it well and tightly. Take another sheet of foil and cover the packet once more.
5. Bake in a preheated oven at 400° F for about 40 minutes.
6. Meanwhile, make the aioli as follows: Add mayonnaise, garlic, salt and pepper into a bowl and mix well.
7. Serve fish and vegetables with a large blob of aioli.
8. Serve right away.

Vegan Pumpkin Risotto

Serves: 6

Ingredients:

- ½ cup leeks, chopped
- 6 cups cauliflower, grated to rice like texture
- ½ cup nutritional yeast
- 4 tablespoons vegan butter or olive oil
- Pepper to taste
- Salt to taste
- 1 cup pureed pumpkin or butternut squash
- 2 teaspoons paprika or to taste
- ½ cup fresh parsley, chopped (option)
- ½ cup vegetable broth or non-dairy milk of your choice

Method:

1. Place a skillet over medium heat. Add vegan butter and melt. Add leeks and sauté until translucent. Add paprika, salt and pepper and stir for a few seconds.
2. Add broth and stir. Add cauliflower and mix well.
3. Cook until the cauliflower turns soft. Stir a couple of times while it is cooking.
4. Add pumpkin puree and mix well. Taste and adjust the seasoning if necessary.
5. Add nutritional yeast and stir.
6. Garnish with parsley and stir.

Vegan Coconut Lime Noodles with Chili Tamari Tofu

Serves: 2

Ingredients:

For noodles:

- 7 ounces canned full fat coconut milk
- 2 tablespoons sesame seeds
- ¼ teaspoon ground or fresh ginger, grated
- Salt to taste
- 1 package (8 ounces) shirataki noodles
- Juice of ½ lime
- Zest of ½ lime, grated + extra to garnish
- A large pinch red pepper flakes, to garnish

For tofu:

- 7 ounces extra firm tofu, drained, pressed of excess moisture, cut into 1" cubes
- ½ tablespoon olive oil
- 2 tablespoons low sodium tamari
- Cayenne pepper to taste

Method:

1. Place tofu in a shallow dish in a single layer. Mix together in a bowl, oil, tamari and cayenne pepper and pour over the tofu. Toss well so that it is well coated.
2. Transfer on to a baking sheet. Spread it in a single layer.

3. Bake in a preheated oven at 350° F for about 20-25 minutes.
4. Meanwhile, drain the noodles. Rinse and add into a wok or skillet.
5. Place the skillet over medium heat. Add rest of the ingredients of the noodles and mix well. Cover the pan partially and cook for 6-7 minutes.
6. Lower heat and cook for 6-8 minutes. Turn off the heat. Cool for a while.
7. Serve noodles on individual serving plates. Place tofu on top. Sprinkle lime zest and red pepper flakes and serve.

Chapter Ten: Dairy-free Ketogenic Dessert Recipes

Easy Chocolate Gelatin Pudding

Serves: 4

Ingredients:

- 2 cups canned, full fat coconut milk
- 1 teaspoon stevia powder extract
- 2 tablespoons gelatin
- 4 tablespoons cacao powder or organic cocoa
- 4 tablespoons water

Method:

1. Add cocoa, coconut milk and stevia into a pan. Place the pan over medium heat.
2. Whisk well. Add gelatin and water into a bowl and mix well.
3. Pour into the pan. Stir constantly until gelatin dissolves.
4. Turn off the heat when the mixture is warm and pour into 4 ramekins.
5. Refrigerate until it set.

Coconut Brownies

Serves:

Ingredients:

For wet ingredients:

- 1 cup organic birch xylitol or 4 teaspoons stevia powder extract
- 1 cup full fat coconut milk
- 2 cups coconut oil, melted
- 2 teaspoons vanilla extract
- 4 eggs

For dry ingredients:

- 1 ½ cups cocoa powder
- 2 cups almond flour, preferably blanched
- 1 cup shredded coconut
- 1 teaspoon baking soda
- 1 cup walnuts, chopped

Method:

1. Add all the wet ingredients into a bowl and mix well.
2. Add all the dry ingredients except walnuts into a bowl and mix well.
3. Pour the wet ingredients into the bowl of dry ingredients and mix until well combined.
4. Add walnuts and stir.
5. Pour batter into a greased, square baking dish.

6. Bake in a preheated oven at 350° F for 30-40 minutes or a toothpick, when inserted in the center, comes out clean.

Low Carb Coconut Cream with Berries

Serves: 2

Ingredients:

- 1 cup coconut cream
- 1/8 teaspoon vanilla extract
- 4 ounces fresh strawberries, chopped

Method:

1. Add all the ingredients into a bowl.
2. Blend with an immersion blender until smooth.
3. Spoon into bowls. Chill and serve.

Triple Layer Choconut Almond Butter Cups

Serves: 6

Ingredients:

For bottom layer:

- ¼ cup cacao paste, finely chopped
- ¼ teaspoon vanilla bean powder
- 2 drops pure almond extract
- 2 tablespoons coconut oil, melted
- ¼ teaspoon ground cinnamon

For middle layer:

- 2 tablespoons coconut oil, melted
- ¼ cup natural almond butter
- 1/8 teaspoon ground cinnamon

For top layer:

- ¼ cup creamy coconut butter
- 2 tablespoons coconut oil, melted

To garnish:

- A little coconut flakes, toasted
- 6 whole almonds

Method:

1. Place parchment paper cups or silicone cups in a 6-count muffin pan.
2. To make bottom layer: Add cacao paste in a microwave safe bowl and microwave on high

for 20 to 30 seconds. Stir and repeat each time for 20 seconds until completely melted.

3. Add rest of the ingredients and mix well.
4. Pour into the prepared muffin pans. Place the pans in the refrigerator for 10-15 minutes or until set.
5. To make middle layer: Add all the ingredients of the middle layer into a bowl and mix well. Pour over the bottom layer in the muffin cups.
6. Place the pans in the refrigerator for 10-15 minutes or until set.
7. To make the top layer: Mix together all the ingredients of the third layer into a bowl.
8. Pour over the middle layer in the muffin cups. Place an almond in each. Sprinkle a pinch of coconut in each muffin cup.
9. Place the pans in the refrigerator for an hour.
10. Remove from the pans and place in an airtight container until use. It can last for many weeks in the refrigerator.

Raspberry Cheesecake

Serves: 8

Ingredients:

- 4.4 ounces creamed coconut milk
- ½ teaspoon vanilla extract or ¼ teaspoon vanilla bean powder
- ¼ cup almond flour
- 10 drops stevia (optional)
- ½ cup frozen raspberries
- 1 tablespoons erythritol or swerve, powdered
- 2 tablespoons coconut flour

For coating:

- 0.7 ounce cacao butter or extra virgin coconut oil
- 1.4 ounces 90% dark chocolate, unsweetened, dairy-free

Method:

1. Add creamed coconut milk, raspberries and erythritol into a blender and blend until smooth.
2. Add almond flour and coconut flour and blend until well combined.
3. Spoon into ice tray, about 1 tablespoon in each well. Freeze for an hour.
4. To make coating: Add coconut oil and dark chocolate into a heatproof bowl. Place the bowl in a double boiler. Stir occasionally until the mixture is well combined.

5. Remove the fat bombs from the ice tray and dip into the chocolate mixture.
6. Place on a tray that is lined with parchment paper. Freeze until set. Transfer into an airtight container.
7. Store in the freezer until use. It can last for many weeks in the freezer.

Pumpkin Spice Fat Bomb Ice Cream

Serves: 12

Ingredients:

- 2 cups pumpkin puree
- 8 yolks from pastured eggs
- 8 whole pastured eggs
- 2/3 cup cacao butter, melted
- ½ cup MCT oil
- 2/3 cup coconut oil
- 4 teaspoons pumpkin pie spice
- ½ cup xylitol or 30-40 drops alcohol free stevia
- Ice cubes, as required (10-15)

Method:

1. Add all the ingredients except ice cubes into a blender and blend until smooth.
2. Add 1 ice cube at a time and blend each time.
3. Pour into an ice cream maker and churn the ice cream following the manufacturer's instructions.
4. Serve immediately if you desire soft serve ice cream.
5. For firmer ice cream, transfer into a freezer safe container.
6. Freeze until firm.
7. Scoop and serve

Conclusion

Thank you once again for purchasing this book! I hope you had an enjoyable and more importantly - an informative read.

I trust this book has helped lay a strong foundation of your understanding of the dairy-free ketogenic diet. I assure you that the recipes are all tried and tested and will help you immensely in keeping your weight under control. The ingredients used in these recipes are all easily available, so you don't have to worry about cooking something with exotic ingredients. It is pretty much food cooked from your everyday ingredients.

Now that you know how to go about it, what effects you should watch out for or expect, along with the dos and don'ts of food followed by all the recipes already nudging you to step into the kitchen – you are fully prepped to venture into your dairy-free keto life.

Best wishes!

Thank you.

Bonus!

Wouldn't it be to know when Amazon's top kindle books go on Free Promotion? Well now is your chance!

I would like to give you full access to an exclusive service that will email you notifications when Amazon' top Kindle books go on Free Promotion. If you are someone who is interested in saving a ton of money, then simply go to the link below for Free access.

http://bit.ly/2097Zgk

As a "Thank you" for downloading this book, I would like to give you "Get The Body Of Your Dreams" ebook.

Resources

https://draxe.com/dairy-free-diet/

https://ketodietapp.com/Blog/post/2015/01/03/Keto-Diet-Food-List-What-to-Eat-and-Avoid

https://ketoschool.com/the-43-health-benefits-of-ketogenic-dieting-in-addition-to-weight-loss-1e4ee4743f1f

https://www.medicalnewstoday.com/articles/180858.php

https://thrivestrive.com/ketosis-signs/

https://www.perfectketo.com/how-to-maintain-ketosis/

Made in the USA
San Bernardino, CA
20 April 2018